ALL ABOUT DONKEYS

CONTENTS

D1740866

The sturdy, smaller relation of the horse, which today we call the donkey, has established a special place in the lives of people since prehistoric times.

The ancestor of the modern donkey lived in wild herds throughout North Africa and many parts of Asia. In North Africa, there were two species of donkeys. The *Nubian* was the shorter, and had a cross-shaped mark on its shoulder. Further to the east was the taller *Somali*.

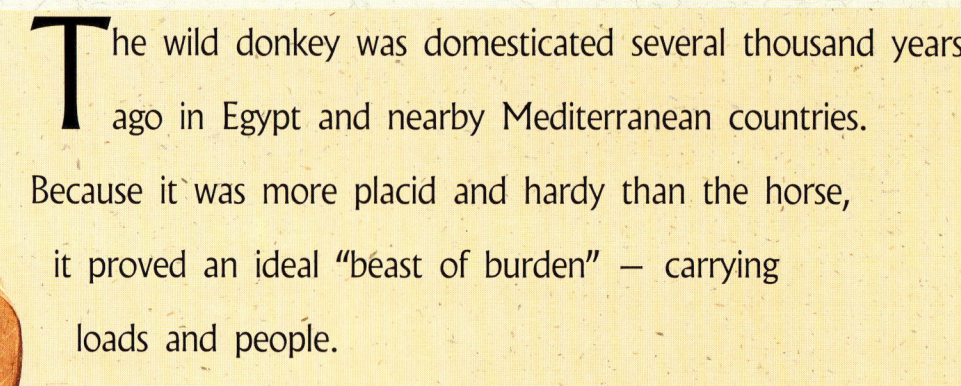

The wild donkey was domesticated several thousand years ago in Egypt and nearby Mediterranean countries. Because it was more placid and hardy than the horse, it proved an ideal "beast of burden" — carrying loads and people.

As donkeys carried goods along the trade routes from one country to another, they gradually spread throughout the Mediterranean into Asia. Eventually they reached Europe, and the Romans took them to Britain almost two thousand years ago.

4

EUROPE

NORTH AMERICA

ATLANTIC OCEAN

MEDITERRANEAN
SEA

ASIA

DONKEY
DISTRIBUTION

NORTH AFRICA

INDIAN OCEAN

ATLANTIC OCEAN

SOUTH AMERICA

0   1000   2000   km
     1000   2000

By the sixteenth century, so many wars had been fought in Europe that horses — the principal animal used by armies — had started to become scarce. In England, Wales, and Ireland, farmers looking for an alternative animal to help them farm their land began to use donkeys.

Donkeys first arrived in the United States in 1868. Brought in by the Spanish-speaking people from Mexico, they were medium-size and known as *burros*. They bred with horses to produce larger, stronger animals called *mules*.

Mules were commonly used by gold miners as pack animals. Explorers would often travel in convoys, which were known as *mule trains*.

When engines for transport and agricultural machinery were developed, the donkey's role as a beast of burden soon ended. The naming of some early machinery, for example the *donkey pump* and *donkey engine,* recognized the donkey's capacity for endurance and monotonous hard work. People today still refer to tedious or hard work as *donkey work.*

As donkeys were not needed any more in most Western countries, their numbers dwindled. A few were used at fairgrounds or to give children rides at the beach, but many were simply left in fields to fend for themselves and became badly neglected.

8

Today donkeys are used for work mainly in the countries around the Mediterranean and in North Africa — the same areas where they were originally domesticated.

DONKEY FACTS

A donkey's height is measured from the ground to the top of its *withers.* As with horses, height is measured in human *hands* (hh). This stems from long ago, when a human hand (10 cm, or 4 in) was used as the basis of measurement.

The largest donkeys come from France. One measured 167.5 cm, or 66 in (more than 16 hh), which is the equivalent of a large horse. Donkeys under 9 hh are uncommon and are known as miniatures. The smallest adult donkey recorded was 61 cm, or 24 in (6 hh).

The average life span of donkeys in England is about 37 years. But in many other countries, working donkeys die before they reach twelve years of age. The oldest recorded age for a donkey is 57 years.

When a donkey calls, it is said to *bray*. Braying makes a sound like *hee-haw*. A male donkey is called a *stallion* or *jack;* a female is called a *mare* or *jenny*. A baby donkey is a *foal*. A male foal is a *colt;* a female foal is a *filly*. In the United States, the mare is often called a *jennet* or *hinny*.

The gestation period, the length of time it takes for a young animal to develop before birth, varies from eleven to thirteen months. Within a few minutes of birth, the foal tries to get to its feet, but it is very wobbly and often falls down. After about fifteen minutes, it is able to stand properly, and it starts to look for food.

12

Most donkey foals have a long fluffy coat and are beautiful, gentle little creatures. Newborn foals are not at all afraid of humans, but after a day or two they become more cautious.

A few days after birth, the first teeth appear, but it will be two years before all the first teeth (milk teeth) are present.

Ideally, a foal should not be weaned and separated from its mother until it is nine to twelve months old.

Donkeys are herd animals and need another donkey, pony, horse, sheep, or goat for company.

A donkey needs at least a quarter of a hectare (half an acre) of grass to provide some of its food and enough exercise. Donkeys which are kept in a smaller area should be walked or ridden.

In wetter and colder climates, donkeys need access to a shelter of some kind.

Donkeys should not get a diet consisting only of grass, as they need plenty of fibrous foods such as hay, straw, and pony pellets. In winter, extra food will be needed. Clean water must always be available. Most donkeys won't drink water that is dirty or stagnant.

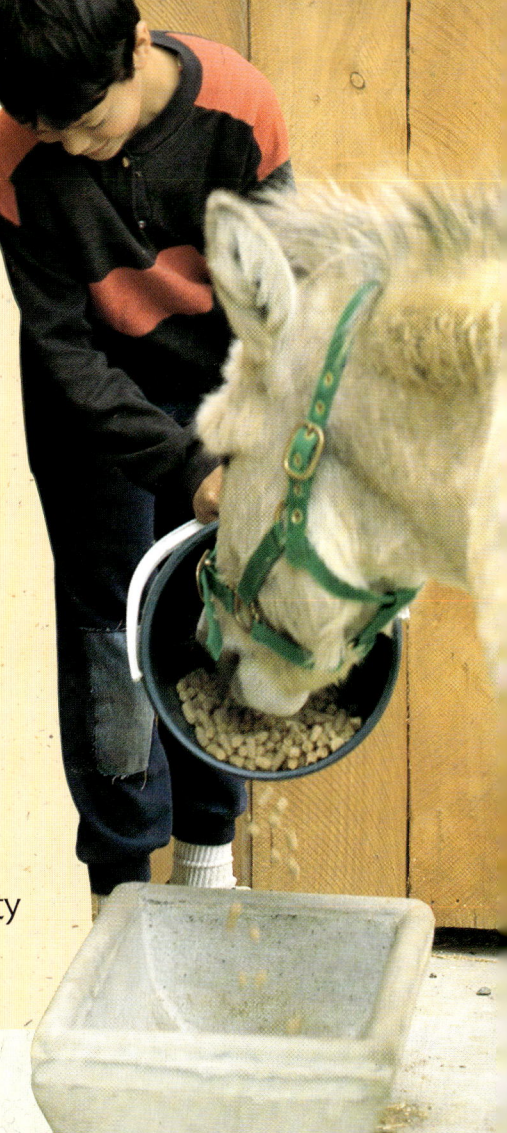

Ideally, a donkey should be brushed every day so the owner can detect any problems, such as cuts or scratches.

A donkey's feet need a lot of care. In wet or muddy conditions, the hard part of the hoof becomes soft. This allows infection to get in under the nail bed and cause a condition known as *seedy toe*.

16

A donkey's teeth grow all the time. If they don't meet properly, they can grow sharp edges, and these will need filing.

Donkeys need regular *drenching* to protect them from intestinal worms. Some worm treatments come in a ready-made syringe.

Lice can infect the coats of donkeys, causing itching. Donkeys roll in dust or rub against posts and trees in an effort to get rid of this itching. This causes bare patches. The treatment is to use a special powder or wash.

A DONKEY SANCTUARY

In 1969, a lady named Elisabeth Svendsen, who lived in Devon, England, and loved donkeys, discovered that many of them were being neglected or cruelly treated. She started to raise the money to buy these donkeys and provide them with somewhere to live. In 1973, she and her husband founded the Southwestern Donkey Sanctuary.

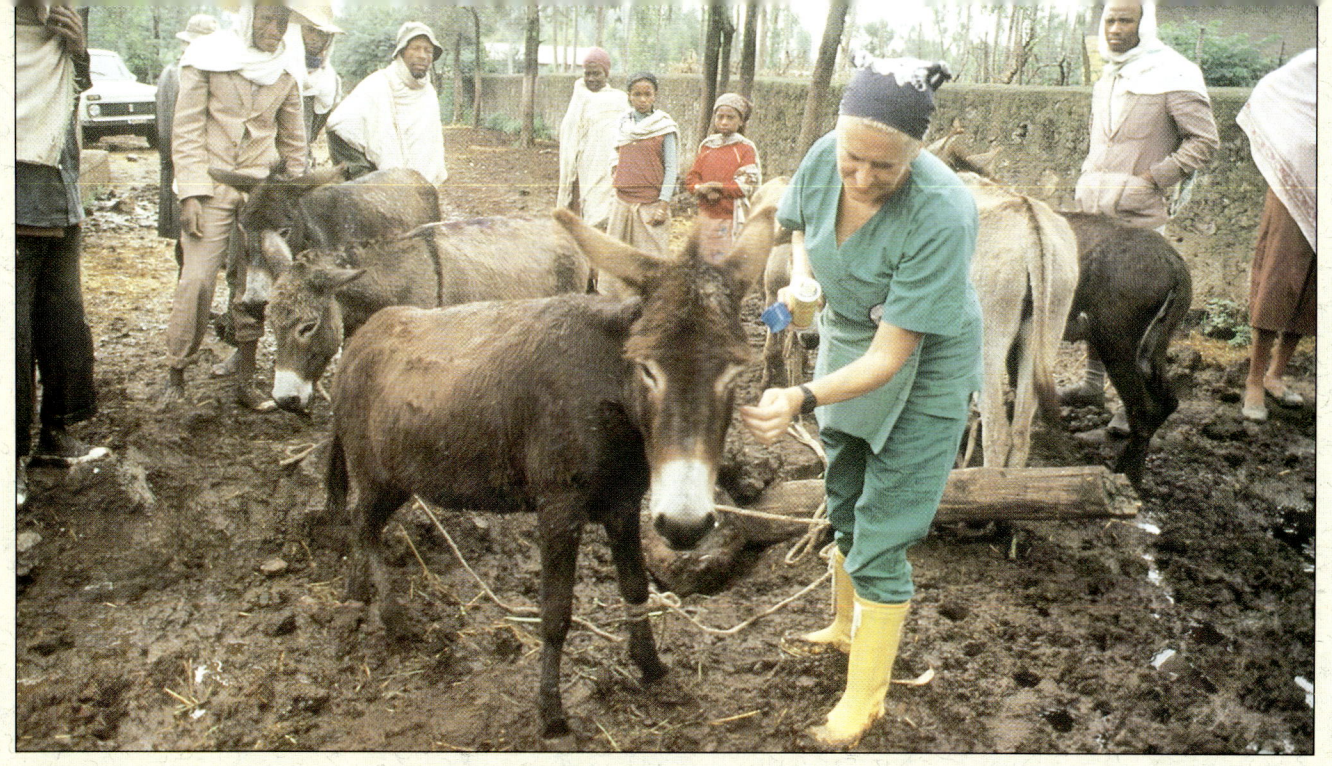

They were inundated with donkeys when an old lady who had another sanctuary left 204 donkeys to the Donkey Sanctuary in her will! The Donkey Sanctuary now cares for more than 4,000 donkeys, and the International Donkey Protection Trust works in many countries to ensure that donkeys are better treated.

At the Slade Centre of the Donkey Sanctuary, physically challenged children learn to ride specially selected donkeys. The donkeys, with their patient, placid natures, are ideal for the children to ride. The children benefit not only from the exercise, but also by their association with these friendly, gentle animals.

Many agricultural shows have classes for donkeys, where the animals can be shown in different ways. They may be led on a long rein, which is called in-hand showing. This type of showing can be done by young handlers.

In ridden classes, the donkeys are saddled and bridled and ridden by children.

There are also driving classes, where the donkeys are in harness.

21

Donkeys have featured in many stories. People of the Christian religion associate donkeys with the Christmas and Easter festivals. (Some say that is why the Nubian donkey has a cross-shaped mark on its shoulder.)

During the First World War at the battle of Gallipoli, a stretcher-bearer named John Simpson Kirkpatrick and his donkey became a familiar sight as, day and night, they brought hundreds of wounded men from the battlefield to safety. Simpson and his donkey became a universal symbol of courage.

DONKEY TALES

The ancient Egyptians made the donkey's head and ears a symbol of ignorance. Someone who behaves stupidly may be told, "Don't be such a donkey".

Perhaps unfairly, donkeys have been characterized as stubborn. In reality, they are courageous, patient animals that are responsive and affectionate when well treated, and in many parts of the world they are still the uncomplaining "beasts of burden" that they have always been.

23

INDEX